'Steam Trains' have been a source of fascination to young and old alike ever since the first railway was opened in the 1830s. Now that electricity and diesel power are replacing steam all over the world it is important to catalogue those fine engines before they completely disappear. Colin Garratt is a photographer of international repute, who also brings to his work a deep affection for this fascinating subject. This book shows locomotives in the deserts of Africa, the jungles of the Far East and in the heart of great industrial complexes, where many of them are still working after half a century.

STEAM LOCOMOTIVES
OF THE WORLD

Text and photographs by COLIN GARRATT

Ladybird Books Loughborough

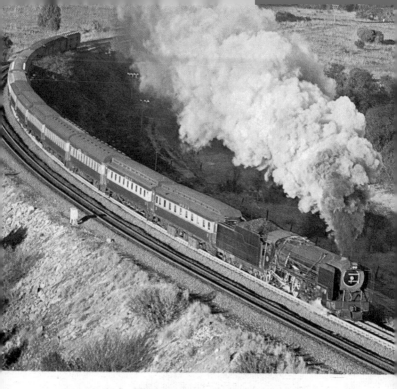

I begin this selection of world engines with one of the finest sights in the history of transport – steam locomotives at speed with heavy express trains. The picture above shows a powerful 4-8-2 storming a gradient of 1 in 100 in South Africa's Orange Free State with a seventeen-coach special from Bloemfontein to Kroonstad.

Opposite we see one of the world's last high speed steam-hauled expresses at work on the Berlin to Dresden main line in Eastern Germany. The engine is one of the famous German O1 Pacific 4-6-2s introduced in 1925 for operating fast trains throughout the country.

Until 1977, these fifty-year-old engines were working trains of 500 tons in weight on timings faster than a mile a minute and they frequently topped speeds of 80 mph. Notice the long windshields for deflecting the smoke clear of the driver's view and also the large driving wheels, 6′ 6¾″ (2000 mm) in diameter, for fast running.

An older type of express passenger engine is repre-
sented by this Pakistan Railway's SPS class 4-4-0
caught hastening away from Malakwal in the Punjab
with a cross-country train. The acrid pall of black smoke
issuing from the engine indicates that she is an oil burner
as there are no coalfields in Pakistan.

Look at the passengers clinging to the sides of the coaches and even riding in the engine's tender! Railways are the principal form of transport in many rural areas of Pakistan; services are often sparse and trains tend to be full. Accordingly the surplus passengers find a place wherever they can.

The SPS class in Pakistan are far from being the oldest passenger engines left in service. This veteran 2-4-0 was built by Sharp Stewart of Manchester in 1885 to a design of 1880 and, along with several sisters, she still works a branch line in Southern Java.

The 2-4-0 was one of the earliest forms of passenger engine; it evolved in Britain during the 1830s and by the first quarter of the 20th century had largely disappeared from the world's railways. It was believed to be extinct and the discovery of this enclave in Java during the 1970s caused much excitement amongst railway enthusiasts.

As the engine wheezes along a rickety weed-strewn branch line, steam pours from her leaking cylinders and shrouds of fire are flung up into the night skies. Look at the chimney top; it is almost like a molten candle. The Indonesian State flags fluttering from the smoke-box are a part of the Independence Day celebrations, as until 1949, these islands were ruled by the Dutch.

Antiquated in the extreme, the engine has no brakes apart from manually operated ones on the tender wheels. However, a combination of old age and poor track restricts speeds to around 15 mph and when the driver wishes to stop he merely shuts off steam! In their heyday, locomotives of the 2-4-0 type achieved some remarkable performances, notably the London & North Western Railway's No. 790 'Hardwicke', which in 1895, covered the 141 miles from Crewe to Carlisle in just over two hours – an average speed of 67.2 mph. 'Hardwicke' is now preserved in the National Collection.

The steam locomotive's evolution was governed by a continuous demand for higher speeds and more power to cope with increasingly heavy trains. Thus the 2-4-0 progressed into the 4-4-0, followed by the 4-6-0 and by the 1920s, the 4-6-2 or Pacific type was in widespread use. Almost a century's evolution can be seen by comparing this engine with the Pacific on the following page.

With a sunset raging across the sky, a Pakistan Railway's XA Class Pacific eases out of the depot prior to taking a train. A full head of steam has caused the engine's safety valves to open – an action which takes place whenever the pressure exceeds the engine's working norm of 180 lbs per sq inch (12.7 kg cm²).

Built by the Vulcan Foundry in Lancashire, this engine is one of the 'X' type standards prepared during the 1920s for the 5′ 6″ (1650 mm) gauge lines of the Indian Sub-Continent.

In contrast, a Pakistan Railway's SPS also raises steam. These 4-4-0s have 6′ 1″ (1854 mm) diameter driving wheels and two inside cylinders and are typical express passenger engines of the late Victorian period.

Despite being over seventy five years old, some of these engines run two thousand miles a week across the Punjab Plains and reach speeds of 65 mph.

The SPSs are a tribute to our forefathers' workmanship; they were introduced by Beyer Peacock of Manchester in 1902, and were supplied when the Indian Sub-Continent was part of the British Empire.

Having seen engines from the British and German schools of design, we find a rare survivor from the Austrian Empire. She is pictured shortly after midnight in a remote goods yard in Slovenia, Northern Yugoslavia.

The rain was beating down as, with a hiss of steam, the clanking engine slid to a halt. The driver jumped out to apply a round of oil to the valve gear. The engine placed two wagons from its train onto the foreground track; a shrieking whistle pierced the air and the veteran wheezed and clanked on through the night.

An industrial antique, she came from the drawing board of the legendary Karl Golsdorf – Chief Mechanical Engineer of the Austrian State Railway from 1891 until his death in 1916. Golsdorf is credited with producing some fifty different classes during his tenure of office and many continued to be built in modified form long after his death.

This engine is a 2-8-0 with 4′ 1½″ (1258 mm) diameter driving wheels for heavy hauling and is an improved version of the Golsdorf 170 Class introduced in 1897.

Italy's railways came under state control in 1905 and within a few years a range of standard classes had been built. All steam locomotive construction in Italy ceased in the 1920s due to the electrification programme. The Italian standards possessed a distinct family appearance and hundreds remained active until the mid 1970s. One of the best known types is the 740 class 2-8-0 freight design of 1911 and one is depicted above bursting from a tunnel in the Dolomite Mountains of Northern Italy.

A midnight scene in a South African goldmine showing a vintage tank engine hauling a load of gold-ore from the mines. Notice how the engine's smokebox is stained white from passing under the loading hoppers.

Built by Dubs of Glasgow during the 1890s, this 4-8-2 worked passenger trains on the Natal Government Railway until being sold to the Grootvlei Proprietary Gold Mines where she remains in regular use.

Now we have seen a selection of conventional engines, the following twelve pages will cover some unusual types designed to fulfil specific functions.

Perhaps the most noteworthy is the articulated four-cylinder Garratt. Here is a member of the Kenyan Railway's 59 Class 4-8-2+2-8-4 Garratts, which are each named after a mountain in East Africa. Thirty four of these metre gauge giants were built by Beyer Peacock

in 1955 for hauling 1200-ton trains from Mombasa on the Indian Ocean up to the Kenyan capital, Nairobi, situated 332 miles inland. During the course of this journey, the trains climb the equivalent of one mile in altitude.

The Harz Mountains of Eastern Germany are one of Europe's most scenic regions. Many visitors to the area ride on the Selketalbahn, a charming metre gauge line using 0-4-4-0 Mallet type tank engines dating back to the turn of the century.

The four-cylinder Mallet is an articulated relation of the Garratt and has two pairs of cylinders driving separate sets of wheels – as the picture clearly shows. The Garratt and Mallet articulateds are discussed on the following page.

The Garratt and the Mallet are the most important articulated steam locomotive types. Both principles enable large engines to be used on steeply graded and tightly curved track.

The two types have independently driven sets of driving wheels. On the Garratt, both sets are articulated, whilst the Mallet has only its leading set articulated – the rear wheels being mounted in a rigid frame as on normal engines. Traditionally, the Mallet is a four-cylinder compound, wherein the steam passes from the boiler to two high pressure cylinders and, instead of being exhausted into the atmosphere, it passes to two low pressure cylinders to do further useful work. The Mallet was extensively used in America and the largest steam engines ever built – the Union Pacific Railway's 550-ton 'Big Boys' – followed the Mallet principle – though not as compounds.

In contrast, the Garratt has its boiler and firebox slung between two independent sets of wheels each driven by two cylinders placed at the outer ends – as the picture on pages 16-17 shows. The engine's water tank is placed over the leading set of wheels and the fuel bunker over the rear set. Apart from the Garratt's ability to negotiate tight curves, the engine's weight is spread over a wide area. This provides a light axle loading in relation to the engine's size and enables it to work over lightly laid tracks and weak bridges.

Patented by H. W. Garratt in 1907, the Garratt locomotive was adopted by Beyer Peacock of Manchester with whom it is commonly associated. The type found particular favour in Africa where many survive today.

This amazing looking engine, seen pulling a trainload of logs in the Philippine Islands, is known as a Shay – a type of engine once used in American lumber forests.

In place of normal driving wheels, the Shay is mounted on several four-wheeled bogies known as trucks; apart from providing articulation, these also spread the engine's weight. The cylinders – mounted vertically on the engine's right hand side – drive a horizontal crank shaft running the length of the engine. This shaft carries pinions which engage with bevelled gears on the bogie wheels to give an even turning movement providing an efficient transfer of power. Speeds are inevitably low and Shays rarely exceed 15 mph.

In common with the Shay, the Crane Engine is also on the verge of extinction and the delightful engine pictured above is probably the last one left in commercial service anywhere in the world. She was built by Manning Wardle of Leeds in 1903 for the 5′ 6″ (1650 mm) gauge

WATER TANK   CAPACITY 3½ TONS

POH DATE 31-5-74
NEXT POH DATE 30-9-77
3

JUD W

lines of India and can be found working today at a
sleeper factory one hundred miles north of the Indian
capital New Delhi. The engine's job is to carry huge
tree trunks into the factory where they are cut into
sleeper lengths for use on main lines.

The engines we have seen so far all generate steam
from their own fires but this amazing veteran – seen
working at a clay plant in Austria – takes her steam
from the factory boilers. One charge enables the 2′ 0″
(600 mm) gauge engine to haul a sixty-ton trainload of
silica clay over a 1½ mile long branch line which
connects with the main railway network. Having delivered the wagons, the engine returns to the factory
with empties and receives a further supply of steam.

The engine is known locally as the 'Wursteldampfer' –
meaning a hot dog machine! She was built in Vienna in
1930 and is possibly the only fireless engine in the world
regularly employed on branch line work.

Fireless engines have been used in Germany since the beginning of the century and were introduced into Britain shortly before World War I. They are beneficial for shunting in such places as paper works and munitions factories where sparks emitted from a conventional engine could have disastrous consequences. However, they also found favour at industrial establishments possessing a ready supply of high pressure steam such as gas works, power stations and various manufacturing industries.

A few still survive today in West Germany, where the largest and most modern examples can be found – some having been built as recently as the early 1970s.

The arid Karroo Desert in South Africa was a forbidding place to build a railway, but the main line northwards from Cape Town had to traverse this expanse. From the outset, difficulties were encountered in obtaining sufficient water for the engines passing through – especially during the dry season. Special trainloads of water had to be taken into the desert and this was a costly and inefficient method of operation.

As traffic increased the problem grew to intolerable

proportions and the railway authorities began consultations with the German firm of Henschel with a view to acquiring some special condensing engines. It was decided that ninety 4-8-4 type engines with condensing tenders should be supplied. The first was built by Henschel in 1953 and the remaining eighty nine came from North British of Glasgow between 1953/4 at a cost of £112,000 each.

Classified 25, the new engines were the ultimate in South African steam power and they quickly revolutionised services through the desert by their ability to run for 700 miles without replenishment of water.

Their method of operating is fascinating. After the steam has driven the pistons, it passes down a large pipe to the 70′ (21.5 m) long tender. En route it drives a turbine to activate five enormous air intake fans situated in the tender top. These draw in cool air through meshing in the tender sides where condensing elements turn the steam to water for recycling into the boiler. Because Condensers have no exhaust heat, the draught required for smoke emission is provided by a turbine-driven fan placed in the smokebox base. Our picture shows the smoke billowing up from the fan's draught and the Condenser's characteristic pear-shaped front. Notice the steam leaking from the condensing elements just above the meshing in the tender sides.

The total length of a 25 Class is 108′ (33.25 m) and they weigh 240 tons in full working order. Many are fitted with roller bearings throughout and once during a gale at Cape Town, one actually blew along the track – so little is the effort required to move them.

CASTLE DONINGTON POWER STATION

C.E.G.B
1

Having discussed unconventional types we return to normality with a selection of small industrial engines.

The engine illustrated above is a typical 0-4-0 Saddle Tank – so named because the water tank fits over the boiler in the shape of a saddle. She is one of the most modern engines in this book, having been built as recently as 1954 by Robert Stephenson & Hawthorn of Newcastle for the Castle Donington Power Station in the English Midlands.

The engine's job is to convey loaded wagons of coal – delivered to the Power Station sidings by the main line railway – up to the conveyors which feed the station's boilers. As we shall see later, this engine's basic design dates back to the turn of the century.

The scene below was on the Anthracite Coalfield near Swansea and shows an 0-6-0 Saddle Tank, built by Peckett of Bristol in 1951, heading a load of empty wagons up to the pitheads in the early hours of the morning. As the engine approaches, plumes of steam swirl up against the night sky; flaming coals bounce along the tracksides and rumbling wagons disappear into the gloom.

Now meet 'Sally' from the Assam coalfield situated in the far corner of north eastern India. 'Sally' – seen invigorating the blue twilight with fire – burns a mixture of wood shavings and slack.

The muddy substance stuck around the smokebox door is cow dung ingeniously applied to the ageing 'Sally' to prevent air from leaking into the boilers.

'Sally' is a member of a distinguished line of Saddle Tanks built for industrial use by Bagnalls of Stafford and engines of a similar shape were built from the 1890s onwards for narrow gauge railways in many parts of the world. She has 7″ (175 mm) diameter cylinders; a driving wheel diameter of 1′ 9½″ (537 mm) and weighs 6½ tons in full working order – a contrast indeed with the 240-ton condensing engines of the Karroo Desert!

Industry was created in Assam during the late 19th century. Those early pioneers created tea gardens and collieries which they hacked out of the jungle. It was inevitable that Staffordshire-built steam locomotives should follow their enterprise.

The Turkish hero, Kemal Ataturk, issued a mandate for the country's first steel works to be built in 1938. Steam locomotives were required to operate within the plant and Britain supplied several Hawthorn Leslie 0-6-0 Saddle Tanks; all remain active to this day. One of their duties is to carry ladles of liquid waste from the steel-making furnaces out to the works' periphery, whereupon the waste is tipped in a molten state down what is known as a Slag Bank.

Dramatic scenes such as these were common during

the earlier days of the industrial revolution.

This engine also has a fine family lineage and is one of a long series of 0-4-0/0-6-0 Saddle Tanks built by Hawthorn Leslie over many years. When the company merged with Robert Stephenson in 1937 the amalgam, known as Robert Stephenson & Hawthorn, continued to build to the old Hawthorn Leslie patterns and a similarity will be found between this engine and the one at Castle Donington depicted on page 28.

A Saddle Tank named 'Empress' slips her way across the Derbyshire Coalfield with a heavy train and sets ablaze grassland and coppice alike.

Friction sparks fly from the spinning wheels, whilst the rush of exhaust from the cylinders draws flaming

coals from the firebed and sends them streaking across the sky like tracer, amid shrouds of gushing steam.

Introduced in 1944, nineteen of these engines were built by Bagnalls for use in collieries and dockland areas.

This delightful tank engine is one of a class used for working light trains on 5′ 6″ (1650 mm) gauge lines in India. India's economy remains largely dependent upon railways and country branch lines freely proliferate.

Look at the colourful embellishments the Indian railwaymen apply to their engines; seldom do two look alike. Notice the chimney's imitation brass cap and the riot of highly saturated hues placed in close proximity as in traditional Hindu Art. The driver's turban, however, indicates that he is a Sikh.

The next few pages are devoted to locomotives at work on various sugar plantations. Sugar constitutes one of the world's major industries and the huge tonnages of cane harvested during the milling season have to be carried to the nearest factory for crushing. Narrow gauge railways invariably offer the most efficient method of conveyance.

Steam locomotives sometimes survive on plantations long after they have disappeared from main line use; indeed some sugar companies use former main line engines which they have purchased at little more than scrap price. Apart from its suitability for working over rough plantation tracks, the steam locomotive offers a remarkable economy by burning what is known as Bagasse – the natural waste product of the sugar cane processing. Bagasse is the shredded fibres of sugar cane after it has been crushed and the juices extracted. After drying, these fibres are made up into large straw-like bales prior to being loaded onto the engine's tender.

The heating power of Bagasse is extremely low and when the engine is working hard two firemen are needed to keep up the steam pressure. But in many sugar-producing lands the cost of labour is well below that of importing or obtaining superior fuels such as coal, oil or wood.

Far out in the plantation a Bullock Cart arrives at the railhead with a load of freshly cut cane. Crushing must be undertaken within twenty four hours of cutting or the moisture content reduces in the heat and likewise the sugar value.

The picture was taken on the Suraya Sugar Plantations in the United Provinces of India and the engine works for a factory owned by an eighty four year old Sikh knighted by the British in the days of the Raj.

What a lovely reminder of Victorian England this chocolate coloured engine is! She was built by Kitson of Leeds in 1900 and is one of the most modern engines at Suraya – the oldest having been built in 1873.

The picture below was taken on Negros Island in the Philippine archipelago where the cane is brought to the railhead by Water Buffaloes known locally as Caribaos. These docile beasts have a placid temperament and are ideal for plodding through the tropical heat with heavy loads. Notice the green leaves on top of the cart; these are the Caribao's food.

The loaded wagons are collected once in twenty four hours and a set of empties left in their place.

Many Philippine sugar plantations were developed during the period of American rule and the engine seen arriving is a 2-6-0 Mogul of typical American styling complete with balloon stack chimney. She was built by the American Locomotive Company in 1921.

This rare antique personifies Disneyland as she sits curling wisps of Bagasse sparks against a sunset in the Philippines. What an incredible engine she is. The two

barrels on top of her boiler contain sand. This drops by
gravity through pipes and falls in front of the wheels to
prevent slipping when the engine is working heavy trains
over damp rails.

That rusty bell adorning her running plate is long since defunct. Bells were a traditional characteristic of American engines and were rung whenever the trains approached crossings and station areas. You can also see the cubes of Bagasse piled up inside the tender (page 41). Sheets of corrugated iron protect the Bagasse from the heavy rains which lash the Philippine Islands during the milling season. Bagasse is inefficient fuel at the best of times, but hopeless if wet!

In contrast, the engine seen above has had much care and attention lavished on her. Known as Dragon No 7 she is from a nearby plantation and was built by Baldwins of Philadelphia in 1928.

The stove pipe chimney and black smoke are evidence that she is running temporarily as an oilburner. This is the normal procedure during the first month of crushing when there is insufficient Bagasse to go round.

Below, a German engine undertakes its workaday chores on a Javan sugar plantation. Java's sugar fields were developed under the Dutch who were never prolific locomotive builders. Accordingly, many of the island's engines originated from Germany. The picture shows an Orenstein & Koppel 0-8-0 tender-tank engine named 'Dieng' after a well known Javan volcano. The name is appropriate, although the engine's large conical-shaped chimney is designed to suppress the emission of fire. Java is noted for its volcanoes and a line of extinct craters can be seen in the far distance behind the train.

One of the most amazing railways I have ever found
was this 2′ 0″ (600 mm) gauge line running through the
jungles of northern Sumatra. The railway's purpose is
to carry stones out of the jungle and deliver them to a

crushing plant where they are turned into ballast for use on the trackbeds of the Indonesian State Railways.

I assumed the stones to be taken from a jungle quarry, but upon arriving at the line I was amazed to discover them being gleaned from the bed of a fast-flowing river by natives diving off wooden rafts. Each diver surfaced with one stone at a time and when the rafts were full, they were brought to the water's edge and the stones loaded into rail wagons. When all wagons were filled, the diminutive engine set off into the jungle, with whistle blaring, through long tunnels of tropical vegetation.

Half way between the river and the crushing plant the line is severed by a steep cable-worked incline. The loaded wagons are hauled up one at a time as a corresponding empty descends. When the two sets of wagons have been exchanged an engine on the higher level continues to the crusher and the lower engine returns to the river with empties.

The picture opposite was made at the base of the incline and you can see the large smooth stones in the wagons. Until recently, the crushing was undertaken by gangs of women and children wielding tiny hammers! It is Alice-in-Wonderland-like operations such as these which provide a few years of borrowed time for these remarkable steam antiquities.

The engine – numbered 105 by the Indonesian State Railways – is an 0-6-0 built by Orenstein & Koppel of Berlin in 1920. Weighing 8 tons, she is similar to many others prepared for industrial narrow gauge railways by this renowned German builder.

Oil-burning steam engines can still be found in the Middle East and this fiery locomotive stands at Der'a on the Syrian-Jordanian border after arriving with an overnight goods train from the Syrian capital, Damascus.

This railway – known as the Hedjaz – is the former pilgrim route to Mecca and was built southwards from Damascus early this century to carry Moslem pilgrims towards their holy city in the Arabian desert.

The line only worked in its entirety for a few years as, during World War I, many sections in the south were blown up by Lawrence of Arabia and they remain abandoned to this day.

However, the northern part of the line through Syria and Jordan remains open and some of the original engines and carriages can still be seen. This handsome engine came from Borsig of Berlin in 1914 and is built to the pilgrim route's unusual gauge of 3′ 5⅜″ (1050 mm).

We have seen the steam locomotive in splendid animation, but the scene below reveals an entirely different facet of our subject's personality. It reminds us that all over the world steam engines are being cast aside in favour of more modern forms of motive power.

The wheel has come full circle for these giant 2-8-8-0 Mallets as they lie abandoned in a remote jungle grave-yard. Slowly the engines will rot their way back into the earth and, in so doing, go the way of their dinosaur counterparts millions of years previously.

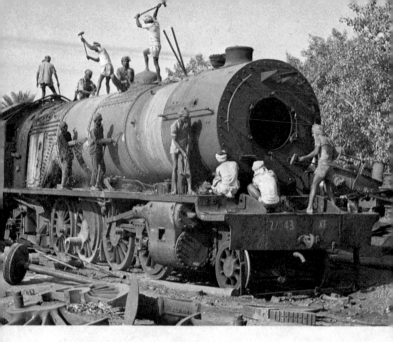

This distressing scene shows the sad end of a British-built XE Class 2-8-2 engine which spent more than fifty years hauling coal trains over the hill regions of India.

Gone now the russet fireglow and clanging shovel; gone the sweet sooty emanations of oil and steam. Fifty back-breaking strokes are needed to knock the head off one boiler rivet, but scrap is vital to a developing India. The foreground is littered with parts of the engine's anatomy – a crank axle, a piston, a dome cover, a chimney, cylinder valves, wheel fragments, springs and a buffer.

And so the trusty steam locomotive, with all its inbuilt simplicity and longevity, is reduced to varying grades of metal for resale at varying market prices.

INDEX